MENDING THE MIRROR

What Science And Medicine Have To Say

About Fixing The Narcissistic Personality –

IN PLAIN ENGLISH

by Alexandra Nouri

Stonington Press, 2013

Contents

A (Fore)Word About Gender

Most destruction by narcissists is wreaked by males. However, there certainly are female narcissists, and they are just as harmful, toxic and hopeless as their male counterparts. If the toad in your life is a female, please simply substitute pronouns as appropriate.

+-+-+

Note: The numerals in parentheses refer to the corresponding cite in the references pages.

+-+-+

Does it pay to hope an abuser is able to change? IS an abuser able to change?

Narcissists are superbly skilled at twisting reality. They are good -- excellent, in fact -- at making their family and partners think the problems in the relationships are because of everyone else. If you are with a narcissist, you've been told that you are the problem, and Aunt Alex will bet a nickel that at least once, you believed it. They said YOU were the one who had issues. YOU were the one who needed to change.

> *You wouldn't like me when I'm angry, because I always back up my rage with facts and documented sources.*
> *– The Credible Hulk*

But the problem with this deceit on their part is that it's so lame that no one believes it for long. Reality has a way of inserting herself into these scenarios eventually. At some point, it becomes clear: This jackass has a problem. A big one. And next, many of people then think: How can we work with it? How can we fix it?

When you break an arm, the doctors and nurses in the emergency room can fix it. When you have depression, there are medications that you can take that help you feel better. So, when a person is diagnosed with a personality disorder, people think, and hope, that there are ways to manage it, to get it under control, even to cure it. After all, it's a disease, and diseases can be helped, right?

Right?

Needless to say, Auntie Alex, as Admiral of Aunt Alex's Army of the Reality-Based, Enlightened, Mighty, Prudent and Emotionally Generous, feels that you should take her word for it: Narcissists aren't fixable, and you can't help them. There's even precious little they can do to help themselves, aside from medicating themselves to oblivion on morphine, 24/7. Their personality disorder is permanent, and you should devote your energy to progressing your own healing and going on to live your own life, fulfilled and narcissist-free.

But, because Auntie loves you and listens to you, she knows it's not easy to do that. These guys work VERY hard to make you care about them and want to bond with them. Just walking away from them without looking back is nearly impossible. Narcissists deliberately pick emotionally generous women, women who give their time, energy, love, money, and futures to people to whom they feel connected. Narcissists know tasty prey when they see it. That emotional generosity makes you refuse to give up easily. Your emotional generosity is a part of you -- you want to help and make things between the two of you work, which is counter to walking away. And maybe you just want some answers about why Auntie thinks she's so right about this incurability thing.

OK. Fair enough.

The truth will set you free, but first it will piss you off. -- Gloria Steinem

So, let's take a walk through what the scientists, doctors, psychologists and other mental and social health professionals have to say about personality disorders, and what the scientific and medical research has borne out.

People have experimented, observed, tried ancient Eastern remedies, created bold new therapies, enforced tough love, prescribed drugs, and stood by and watched while narcissists were given massive doses of love, reassurance, patience, and guidance, for years. For decades. Aunt Alex has gone to the front lines, gathered the data, and sorted it out. The results are consistent, clear, and resonant: Narcissists are screwed up beyond belief, and there's nothing anyone can do that will change that. Now, let's take a look at the landscape of ways to improve the quality of life for people with personality disorders, and the quality of life for people who have to put up with narcissists. Let's find out what works, and what doesn't.

The truth does not change according to our ability to stomach it. -- Flannery O'Connor

First, our understanding of personality disorders is actually fairly new. Depression and anxiety have been identified and studied for many centuries. Personality disorders, on the other hand, were, for a very long time, called "character problems". Narcissists were "wooden" or "shallow"; antisocial types, were "evil"; borderline or schizoid types, were "possessed". Within the last 120 years, scientists, doctors and psychologists started seeing how much the personality disorders have in common and started thinking of them as a group of really badass mental illnesses, and then, later, considered them to be rigid and pervasive mental disorders. The personality disorders were called neuroses, and were studied and explained by J.L.A. Koch, Emil Kraepelin and Sigmund Freud before being brilliantly researched and understood by the psychiatrist Karen Horney in the 1940's (19). After Dr. Horney laid the groundwork, other researchers such as Theodore Millon quickly organized and developed the information the research was generating. They called them personality disorders (rather than regular mental illnesses), because the traits and characteristics ran so deep and the disturbances were so unmoving, that they clearly were unlike any other mental illness -- those traits and disturbances were a part of the very flesh and fiber of the patients themselves. These patients were then called the personality disordered. (Before this, they were, as a population, called "insufferable bastards".) And a new understanding of abusers was born.

Scientists, doctors, and psychologists want to be able to fix personality disorders. They want this a lot. They love helping people, and they love being able to say they can fix things. It's why they picked those jobs, so they could fix things that are really hard to fix, and be proud of their ability to do that. So, they've been trying hard to fix personality disorders for many decades. Everyone, even the most hopeful of practitioners to the most delusional scientists, agree that personality disorders are nasty beasts to treat. They all agree that it's not like medicating panic attacks, or treating trauma with therapy. Most agree that the narcissist wasn't "born mentally normal and had bad things happen to him that caused the mental and emotional disturbance", but instead was born with a personality disorder knit tightly among the neurons and fibers in his brain. This makes treating a personality disorder about as handy as treating profound developmental delay (formerly known as mental retardation), or treating being dead. Also, there is a logistical problem with helping and fixing people with personality disorders: One must get a person with a personality disorder to admit they have a problem. Out of every hundred narcissists, maybe thirty will admit they have a serious problem. And of those thirty who do, good luck getting them to do anything about it. Maybe four will lift a finger in response to this awareness. And of that small fraction, good luck getting them to commit to real change, stick to treatment, and see things through. (The number of successes at that, thus far, worldwide, is currently hovering around zero.) The integrity and consistency required to do that, to commit to change and walk the talk, just are not a part of the narcissist. Even if they do get into long-term therapy, the best you can hope for is the therapy helping to manage very specific, very immediate symptoms like suicide attempts or violent reactions. You can't make personality disordered patients normal. You can't get a troll to grow a soul.

Do you have strong feelings of "I can do this, I can fix this"? Those feelings are diagnostic of a dysfunctional and royally screwed-up relationship. If you sense something needs to be fixed, and that you're the only one who'd be doing the fixing, that's a red flag of epic proportions. -- Aunt Alex

The public, and even some doctors and therapists, don't hear much about how effective treatments are (or aren't) with narcissists. This is because it's not talked about very much, even behind closed doors. Everyone wants to hope, to achieve, to win, and everyone wants to fix problems and do the impossible. But with the therapies that are used, there's no change in the narcissist's love for lying; there is no new ability to empathize, no stability in their wildly swinging moods. It doesn't make them relate better, or bring their thinking closer to reality. The narcissist's core disorder remains unscathed, and the only benefit is that the therapist and the patient both get to say they're trying -- even though nothing in the patient's pathology is changing.

Personality Disorders 101, and Why "Helping" is "Hurting".

Behold, the Parade of Toads, as perceived by mental health professionals.

There are four "drama" types. There is a lot of overlap among these (14).
1. Narcissistic Personality Disorder. All personality disorders feature self-serving lies and bizarre internal chatter, but narcissists take this to a whole new level. Narcissists also tend to be grandiose, exploitive of others, obsessed with appearances, shallow, living in their own fantasy world, and supremely selfish.
2. Borderline Personality Disorder. Borderline types are in very poor control of their emotions; they are impulsive, delusional, prone to making shallow threats, and usually rageful. The ultimate "drama queens" of the personality disorder world.
3. Histrionic Personality Disorder. Histrionic types tend to be exhibitionists; they're seductive, hypochondriacal, immature,and "needy".
4. Antisocial Personality Disorder. Think crime, though you don't have to be arrested to be a criminal (16). Callous disregard for others, for rules, and for morality; usually quick to become rageful; enjoys hurting others, physically and/or emotionally. Lies easily. Either they don't understand that there is a right and a wrong, or they entirely don't care.

It matters not whether you win or lose;
what matters is if *I* win or lose.
-- Darin Weinberg

There are three "odd" types. They also have no ability to empathize and have very poor ego function, but are more likely to have problems just getting along in society, never mind having healthy relationships.

1. Schizoid Personality Disorder. Think "unapproachable loner" type. Maintaining a physical and emotional distance from others, including family, is critical. Never chats or goes out to socialize. Chilly and indifferent.

2. Schizotypal Personality Disorder. More similar to actual schizophrenia. Can be obsessed with things like aliens or visions. Odd behavior. Doesn't trust others, even caring family.

3. Paranoid Personality Disorder. Always thinks he or she is right, and others are trying to harm (cheat, fool, or hurt) them. Conspiracies ruin their lives. Trusts no one; likely to line apartment windows with tin foil or live "off the grid" for survivalist reasons. Grandiose and delusional.

Three "anxious" types exist. These types also cannot empathize, are poor at organizing thoughts and feelings, and have disastrous relationships, and their "uptight" presentation is notable.

1. Avoidant Personality Disorder. The most isolating of all the personality-disordered. Terrified of social interaction, due to their self-loathing and fear of being judged or ridiculed. Prefer to spend their lives living with parents, and barely interacting even with them.

2. Dependent Personality Disorder. This personality type seeks out dominant, narcissistic types to make decisions, care for them, and "lead the way". Likely to feel generally incompetent, wobbly, and weak, regardless of the reality. Like all personality-disordered, dependent types are shallow, delusional, and have dysfunctional relationships.

3. The third "anxious" type is Obsessive-Compulsive Personality Disorder. This is NOT to be confused with obsessive compulsive disorder (OCD). Nothing grates on Aunt Alex's nerves more than confusing these two very different conditions. OCD is a "typical" mental illness, where

patients engage in repetitive or excessive behaviors in order to soothe their anxieties. Obsessive-compulsive personality disorder makes OCD look downright cute. Persons with obsessive-compulsive personality disorder are rageful, delusional, and sadistic. Their type is obsessed with rules – both the written kind, and the kind that exist only in their turbulent minds. They feel what they do is perfect and orderly, and that others are faulty and unacceptable. Their need for control over their surroundings is desperate and all-consuming. Rigid and pedantic.

Life hardly ever lives up to our anxieties. -- Paul Monash

Narcissists and antisocial types dish out abuse easily, and lash out; borderline types tend to have no emotional control whatsoever, and do self-destructive things. Obsessive-compulsive types adhere ridiculously strictly -- and abusively -- to rules, including rules that they themselves make up and could change at any time. The various types help to organize what one can expect from patients based on their diagnosis. For example, if we can peg a narcissist as a narcissist, we know he's going to want to show off and be thought of as unique and fabulous. However, he might not necessarily have the social panicking of an avoidant personality.

What's more compelling, though, isn't how personality disorder types are different from one another, which in some ways is more or less arbitrary, but in the consistent and disturbing ways the patients are alike.

Conduct of the unfit seems always to be inappropriate and unnatural; either disdainful or cringing; either hotheaded or too deliberate; either domineering or fragile; either self-satisfied or sheepish. The fit person avoids extremes.
-- Lao Tzu, Tao Te Ching

There are several types of personality disorders, but they all have much in common. Dominating these commonalities is an in-born deficiency in their brains. Because of this brain deformity, they all are in constant distracted-addict mode, seeking relief from searing inner psychic pain by expressing their type's behaviors, whether it's avoiding all social contact like an avoidant type or threatening suicide as a borderline type. All of the personality disorders seek to hoard as much control over situations as possible in order to help balance out the wildly destabilized internal feelings of impulsivity and fear. All personality disordered people can be abusive and psychopathic, but the "drama" types really excel at it. (The obsessive-compulsive types share membership in that department as well.)

All personality disordered people want to FEEL BETTER. NOW. The various disorder types just describe how the personality disordered, as individuals, tend to do that.

For all patients, the drill goes like this:

1. The personality disorder causes wildly distorted, confusing, and conflicting thoughts and feelings in his head.

2. This chaos in his head causes an extremely high level of anxiety.

3. This sky-high anxiety hurts. The patient feels pain. He doesn't know why; he just knows he is in searing pain.

4. The personality disorder type (narcissistic, avoidant, histrionic, etc.) determines what the patient will probably do to try to make the pain go away so he can feel better.

The personality disordered don't feel the pain coming from within, so they assume it's coming from around them -- their family, their associates, the weather, the world. If you treat the symptoms of a particular type, like the impulsivity of a borderline type or the criminal psychopathic thinking of an antisocial type, the patient is still left with that eternal well of pain and anxiety that delivers a constant supply of internal distress. The observable trait, the impulsivity or the crime, was only the reaction to the chaos in his head, not his environment, or his issues with his childhood, or his not knowing how to say please and thank you.

Those with personality disorders are very ego-centric; they don't bond, and are not team players (2). They can't handle constructive advice, don't love, aren't professional (28), and aren't trustworthy.

All have interpersonal and emotional disasters regularly. They are deceptive, grandiose, shallow, irresponsible, and impulsive. They have no clue about empathy. Even the dependent types need to feel in control (17). Their egos are as fragile as soap bubbles, and they can become emotionally unglued at the slightest hint of criticism. Their ability to modulate their feelings and inner control is pathetic.

When I played pro football, I never set out to hurt anybody deliberately -- unless it was, you know, important, like a league game or something.
-- Dick Butkus

15

People with personality disorders don't trust other people, because for decades, other people have, to the narcissist's thinking, failed to make them feel better. Narcissists aren't just avoiding the criticism of others; they are trying to avoid any additional pain in the ego area, because they are already taking on more than they can handle by having a personality disorder. A disconnected sense of self hurts, because the anxiety is so intense and unrelenting. It hurts like losing a loved one, getting fired, and having your house burn down, all in the same day. It hurts this way all the time. Panic and chaos and trauma, all day long, every day. They even dream in tears and anxiety. (You may pity them from a distance, but don't even think of starting to feel sorry for them, dear readers. They manipulate because of pain, so they can feel like they "win", but they still manipulate. They lie so they can feel "safe", but they still lie. There are starving children and homeless families in every state and every country. Focus your heart's energies on them instead.)

A narcissist's life is a whirlwind cycling of trying to soften the internal pain by putting it onto others (externalizing it), and perceiving other people's words and deeds as incoming attacks, which make him amp up the bad behavior so he can feel a sense of vindictive triumph. This never ends. It can't. He doesn't have the brain strength to end it. The patient's self isn't available to respond to therapy. He can't self-reflect, consult a conscience, feel compassion, or assess incoming information using a set of human values. There is no "there" there. This is, ironically, the best thing for the narcissist (and the worst thing for everyone who has to deal with him), because if he could introspect, and be familiar with himself, he'd be so alarmed and distressed at the emptiness in there, that he'd likely have a psychotic break. Depth of feeling and thought give normal people comfort and growth. For the narcissist, who has missing brain parts, just the idea of such a thing is terrifying. Alienation from his sense of self relieves the tension of the moment, and this is all a personality-disordered person ever wants. Numbness, relief, and instant gratification. A fleeting sense of power and acceptance. He can't get fixed, or introspect, or feel better, or organize his thoughts and feelings. So he grabs onto any immediate ego-feed that he can. It's lame, and it bears only a passing resemblance to healthy human functioning, but to him, it'll do for **right this second**.

We, the public, and mental health professionals, shouldn't mess with this lightly. We all may have the best of intentions when we want to help a narcissist to be a better person. But if we engage in a therapy that seeks to strengthen the "real self" within the narcissist, a raging inner battle of epic proportions can ensue, because people with personality disorders don't have the brain parts to help them organize, modulate, and stay calm about feelings and thoughts. The narcissist isn't prepared to bear the tension and the pain of growth and improvement. His self-loathing and his desperate fear of the primitive pain are the furnace fueling his defenses, which, as a narcissist's family can tell you, have an inexhaustible energy. The power and capacity of his self-hate are astounding. He has a survival interest in NOT exploring, confronting, or resolving a personality disorder, because then he doesn't also have to deal with the self-contempt he'd see when he looked at how empty he felt inside. He would rather pretend the pain comes from other people; other people are a LOT easier to hate, to escape, and to judge. His torments come from within, and he behaves as though they're coming from all around him. This shows you how nasty that internal landscape really is, when you see how hatefully he lashes out at the innocent people around him. He's battling the feelings inside himself with all that viciousness.

Narcissists never move beyond this need for safety. They can never move toward living a truly happy life. They never feel safe long enough to let themselves do so.

To the personality-disordered, other people exist to serve their needs. All narcissists feel entitled to fulfillment of their needs without reciprocity. This feels very natural to them, and it's a perspective that's as unmoving as it is delusional. Encounters with others are turned into competitions, or regimes, or intrigues. Love is quite out of the question; the ability to love is contained in that part of the brain that's missing in the personality-disordered. Besides, narcissists are so intensely, desperately focused on relieving their internal anxiety, that caring two twigs about anyone else is quite impossible. Foiling others makes narcissists feel like they have a shard of control over their lives, and they do it a lot. So, harming or avoiding others, or becoming self-servingly enmeshed with others, feels momentarily good to narcissists; bonding with others or feeling expected to care about them feels unacceptably risky. This tends to have a disastrous effect on relationships.

Every craving we feel is a barrier that keeps contentment just out of reach.
-- Lao Tzu, Tao Te Ching (translation by Richard Degen)

Personality-disordered behavior helps the patient to feel better, to feel like they have successfully avoided excruciating anxiety even if just from fleeting moment to fleeting moment. Narcissists do whatever they have to at any given moment to make themselves feel more safe, and less anxious. This solution, pathetic and maladaptive though it may be, is not going to be relinquished without a fight. The narcissist can't feel liberated by the removal of a protective shield, a comforting blanket, when the outer world feels so threatening and confusing. And the outer world can't seem friendlier and more rational when part of your brain is incorrigibly malfunctioning.

We'll look at the different therapies and treatments used

18

for personality disorders, in detail. Then, we ourselves can understand why they don't work, and we then don't have to just take a skeptic's word for it. Here, in reality, we must call them <u>Ineffective Treatments</u>. This is for a reason. Outside of the Guild of Mental Health Professionals, the word "treatment" suggests that something is being done that actually works, or could work. But among scientists and therapists, "treatment" just means something is being done, whether it works or not. An oatmeal poultice is a "treatment" for depression. You apply it to someone's forehead, and voila -- it's a treatment. It doesn't matter that it doesn't do anything besides gunk up your hair. It is still a treatment. Standing outside in your pajamas and screaming at the ground is a "treatment" for getting rid of mice and moles, even if it doesn't make a damn bit of difference. So, we'll keep it real here, and refer to the various methods as they are -- treatments, but ineffective ones.

Ineffective Treatment #1: Dialectical Behavior Therapy, or DBT

If you've ever looked into how you can possibly save your relationship with a narcissist, you've probably heard of DBT. It is widely considered to be the go-to therapy for people with personality disorders. DBT was developed by a psychologist, Marsha Linehan, in the 1990's (36). The 'D' in DBT stands for 'dialectical', which is related to the word dialog. However, an easier way to understand DBT is to think of the 'D' as standing for "double", because DBT has two main parts working together: mindfulness, or calm awareness, and behavior therapy, or changing your thoughts and feelings by changing your behavior. DBT seeks to improve a person's ability to tolerate distress, so they can respond to stressful situations by reasonably dealing with them rather than spiraling down into a shrieking, raging, irrational, crying, whining, reactive, threatening freak. DBT work addresses the 'here and now', as opposed to sorting out childhood experiences or abstract connections in one's thinking. DBT is very patient-friendly, as it involves lots of acceptance and validation.

DBT is a great therapy approach. It can help almost anyone with mild to moderate anxiety or depression. It can even help with a couple of symptoms of borderline personality disorder, like reducing the frequency of the patient's suicide attempts, or the frequency of his cutting or other self-harm (36). But, that's it. Seriously -- that's the extent to which it can help people with personality disorders (6). The reason DBT is so celebrated in its use with personality disorders, the reason it is used so widely, is because this tiny dent it can make in some borderline patients' behavior, is far more than any other therapy can do for them. Other approaches pretty much do nothing except give the narcissist more tools and ammo with which to manipulate others, **including the therapist**.

Facts do not cease to exist just because they are ignored.
-- Aldous Huxley

Marsha Linehan, the brains behind DBT, is pretty honest and straightforward about DBT's limitations. The tiny results available to the personality disordered are only offering some type of symptom management (6). They don't include real, meaningful changes in the narcissist, or in anyone's ability to put up with them. Minor symptom management is the best we can do. And Marsha Linehan's acknowledgement of this reality is admirable.

Personality-disordered patients cured with DBT: **Zero.**

Ineffective Treatment #2: Schema Therapy

Schema therapy is an approach that clumps together all sorts of other treatments. Cognitive behavioral therapy, Gestalt therapy, skills training, and other approaches all get blended together, and schema therapy aspires to take the best of all of them and do magical things with tough cases -- as with narcissists. A "schema" is like a lens through which patients see the world, and schema therapy seeks to refocus screwy lenses to bring the patient in closer alignment with reality (13). That way, the patient can feel less of the anxiety that was caused by the screwy, "maladaptive" beliefs and perceptions, and behave better and feel better (54). It's a "Tell me about your childhood!" approach.

In healthy people, a change in mood or thoughts or feelings is usually fairly smooth and happens for a reason (4). In narcissists, these changes are a mess. Shifting emotional gears, and feeling things with some degree of balance, is so difficult that it's nearly impossible. Schema Therapy assumes that this is because of bad experiences in childhood, rather than because of permanent, inborn errors in anatomy and body chemistry (54).

It's pretty likely that any given narcissist had a crappy childhood. This is because narcissism, like most other inborn conditions, tend to be inherited from one or both parents. A patient with a personality disorder probably had a parent with a personality disorder, and as any child of a narcissist or antisocial or borderline type can tell you, this is pure, unadulterated hell. What came first, the chicken or the egg? Well, in this case, it's the personality disorder that came first, before the childhood abuse. The narcissist wasn't born normal, and then damaged by a bad childhood. The narcissist was born damaged, and the bad childhood was just a side-serving of crap risotto on the narcissist's plate of a horrible life.

A fit person acts unobtrusively and does not leave tracks by demanding recognition; articulates advice clearly and does not cause confusion; renders to all what is due them so that no one feels cheated; locks no one out of knowledge... so none can claim to have been denied; binds no one through imposition of dogma yet secures minds through good example.
-- Lao Tzu, Tao Te Ching (translation by Richard Degen)

The narcissist certainly has a solid, rigid way of thinking that discards, rejects, or actively and violently denies any challenge to its ideas ("I am supreme and unique", "all others exist only to support me", "I'm too good for you", etc). This is because if his way of thinking gets challenged and collapses, if his defenses fall, he's left with a very poorly constructed psyche that may very well lapse into psychosis.

The narcissist isn't a fully intact, vulnerable person trapped behind some nasty behaviors. He's a fractured, handicapped, disabled sap who pretends to be whole. He's not whole. He's not even salvageable. He's not handicapped in a way that you can think of a "system" to work with his dysfunction. He's not fractured in a way that can be splinted. He is brain damaged, from birth, and the science offers evidence of this, too. We'll cover this thoroughly. First, we'll continue to review why therapies don't work against this brain damage.

A narcissist behaves monstrously badly because he has intense emotions and thoughts and doesn't know what to do with them. His thoughts are immature and don't make much sense, and his emotions are uncontrolled and disorganized. In other words, he's a mess. But trying to help him to calm down, or to manage his feelings, or to grow up, will fail. Because of his disorder, he feels like any work on being a better person would be giving in, surrendering, handing over his humanity to someone else. It's all very paranoid, and that paranoia helps the narcissist to evade the soul-crushing feelings of helplessness and vulnerability that are actually coming from the personality disorder. Does he have these traits only because the right person hasn't come along yet to teach him what he needs to know? No. He has them because he's brain damaged (34). His gears aren't just stuck; they're rusted solid.

We don't devote enough scientific research to finding a cure for jerks. – Bill Watterson

Jeffrey Young, the psychologist who developed schema therapy, reports that personality-disordered patients respond "extremely well" to schema therapy (54). His colleague, D.P. Bernstein, took this even a step further, and reports that schema therapy can help personality disordered patients RECOVER, because, he believes, the disorder is formed by childhood abuse (5). However, scientific and medical literature offers up an astonishingly scarce amount of agreement. Where are the success stories? Where are the recovered patients and their extremely grateful family members, and why aren't they coming forward touting this as the miracle the developers are saying it is?

Maybe some mental health professionals are so amped up and so starved for some tiny improvement, any improvement, in narcissists who are in treatment, that they are a bit loose with their definitions of "improvement" and "recovered". A robustly successful treatment would have case studies and research and lots of reports. Schema therapy doesn't have any more of these than any other treatment, including the oatmeal-on-the-forehead treatment for depression. So, what's going on? Why are the people who have a relationship with narcissists being given so much false hope?

Scientists, doctors, psychologists and other therapists want badly to help people with personality disorders. They want to come up with something that is effective. The benefits of an effective treatment would be huge. Huge. If personality disorders were cured, we'd have a sharp reduction in crime, a healthier society, fewer divorces and break-ups, and an improved quality of life for almost everyone on the planet. (Imagine how different the world would be if every narcissistic leader of a nation, a religion, or a philosophy could be cured of their narcissism.) This pursuit of a cure is understandable. Mental health professionals, therapists and scientists alike, have a certain amount of peer pressure and other human frailties. This can make mental health professionals much too optimistic about treatments for narcissists. It can make them more optimistic than the facts and the data can justify.

    With narcissists and other personality disordered patients, noncompliance and quitting therapy are common (47). The motivation for meaningful change is low. All attempts to soften the narcissistic traits will be met with solid resistance. Just as problematic is the research itself. Experiments with drugs, therapies, and treatments are extremely hard to design for narcissists (44). The problem is in how to measure improvement. Narcissists lie as easily as they breathe. One official scientific study actually gave the borderline patients questionnaires at the end of the study, and used their answers as evidence that the treatment was successful (30).

The secret of success is sincerity. Once you can fake that, you've got it made.
--Daniel Schorr

    Narcissists charm and seduce. Their self-reports about improvement are rarely reliable. Any observable change in their behavior is very unlikely to be a substantial gain, and much more likely to be an in-the-moment blip for the sake of appearances.

    Having said that, it's good that scientists and doctors keep trying, and it's good that they keep talking about wanting to cure, improve, treat and succeed. We just need them to be more honest: Successfully treating narcissistic personality disorder, or any personality disorder for that matter, is not currently possible, and, because of the way it's woven into the person's body and being, would be as dangerous to the patient's ability to cope with life as it would be hopeful. There is no evidence, none, supporting any effective treatment for personality disorders, and the Guild of Mental Health

Professionals need to be consistent and honest with themselves and the public about this.

Confirmed cases of narcissism successfully managed or cured using schema therapy: **None**.

Big egos are big shields for lots of empty space.

-- Diana Black

Ineffective Treatment #3: Cognitive Behavioral Therapy, or CBT

It's been recognized for some time now, about 15 years, that CBT doesn't do anything for personality disorders (33). Rational Emotive Behavioral Therapy, for example, seeks to moderate the harsh ways in which rigid beliefs can control a person. Rigid beliefs are part and parcel of a narcissist's life. It's easy, therefore, to see how doctors and therapists can speculate whether it would work to take the edge off malignant narcissism. But this thinking ignores the overwhelming power of the defenses in personality disorders. It also ignores how those rigid beliefs are created by the personality disorder to compensate for the narcissist's inability to moderate his emotions and thoughts. The personality disorder is what the narcissist has instead of a soul, instead of... a personality. The narcissist is only going to do things to help himself if those things are comfortable AND easy. Meaningful change, and treatment, are neither comfortable nor easy. A narcissist would have to change an enormous amount to be within the healthy range of behaving, thinking, and general functioning. He surely isn't going to change that enormous amount by talking about his childhood or pretending to think about others.

CBT therapists tend to think that behavior is determined by the person's environment (5). If it were that simple, all the children within a family, or students within a classroom, would behave very similarly. Actually, a person's traits and personality have a greater effect on what their behavior will be. Personality disorders aren't just a sack of traits like anxiety, grandiosity, paranoia, etc., that can be sorted out and treated one by one. It's a tightly bound, cohesive mess that fights off all attempts at assistance as though they were poison.

And indeed, to narcissists, such attempts to treat their disorder are poisonous and highly suspect. If you threaten to take away a narcissist's grandiosity, you are threatening to take away their handhold on reality, the one thing keeping them from having a psychotic break. You're threatening to take away that which keeps his self-loathing at bay long enough to allow him to walk, talk, and dress himself. Knowing that, it's no wonder narcissists have no intention of following through with treatments or therapies. It's no wonder they hate the very suggestion.

Examples in the scientific literature of successes using CBT with narcissists: **Zero**.

[With abuse], the whole thing becomes like this evil enchantment from a fairy tale, but you're made to believe the spell can never be broken. -- Jess C. Scott

Ineffective Treatment #4: Skills Training

"He just needs to be taught, lovingly, how to behave." Anyone who says this about a narcissist is invoking the treatment of skills training. Calming himself, speaking appropriately in social situations, inhibiting his impulses, etc., are all skills that people with "simpler" mental illnesses such as anxiety or Asperger's Syndrome can learn. Learning these skills means patients can enormously improve their quality of life, because they WANT to succeed socially, but are unable to deal with things like body language and other social cues which normal people can process instinctively (41). Skills training can include desensitization, relaxation techniques, and good old-fashioned classroom-like lessons in how to act. Patients are able to learn these things because they want to learn them. They have a goal of getting along better with others, and so they take action.

Not so the narcissist. He has no interest whatsoever in getting along with others; he only wants to exploit them for whatever he wants, right that second, at any given time. He can't empathize, or have compassion for others, for the same reason fish can't ride bicycles: he doesn't have the functioning parts. If one assumes that narcissists fail to behave appropriately only because they were never taught how, they are operating under a very weak understanding of personality disorders. A narcissist's deficits and compromises run far deeper and wider than just problems with good manners and "people skills". Empathy and compassion cannot be taught. Bonding and love cannot be taught. One can teach how to mimic these things a little better, or how to memorize responses to certain social situations, but the underlying disorder and its conflicts, anxieties, disturbances, self-loathing, distortions, and externalizations all remain untouched. Any new skills only end up as additional tools narcissists can use to manipulate people.

Narcissists aren't all that teachable. Skills? They don't get it. Examples in the scientific literature of successes using skills training with narcissists? **Nothing**.

Why do you hasten to remove anything which hurts your eye, while if something affects your soul you postpone the cure until next year? -- Horace

Ineffective Treatment #5: Medication

Medication was the most promising of treatments for personality disorders, because it got closer to the root of the problem -- the patient's biological chemistry and brain function. Lots of drugs have been suggested and tested for use with narcissists over the years, and there are few guidelines for medicating personality disorders, other than just prescribing drugs to treat whatever symptom is the main complaint (38). It is very difficult to conduct a good study showing the effects of medications on narcissists, because they almost always drop out, fail to comply with the dosing, or lie about how they are feeling or behaving when asked. When you are treating a personality disorder with medication, you are treating symptoms, like anxiety and depression (40), and not treating the lack of compassion, lying, grandiosity, disjointed thinking, etc. That is, you are not treating the personality disorder.

Antidepressants have been prescribed to narcissists (29). Antipsychotics are usually included. Mood stabilizers and anti-anxiety drugs, too. Hallucinogens have been tried; so have narcotics. Doctors have to be careful about what they prescribe to people with personality disorders, since the potential for narcissists, antisocial patients, borderlines types, etc., to abuse and become addicted is very high, and the potential for their good compliance with the dosing schedule is poor (35). Sometimes, when given these drugs, the patient feels a little better, but their narcissism goes untouched (38). They still are horrible partners, family members, and associates. They're still personality disordered.

There are no findings by scientists or doctors suggesting meds can treat personality disorders. We can't drug a narcissist into being real, or rational, or at peace, or compassionate. Drugs never slow down their manipulations or devaluation. **Drugs don't work**.

It is difficult, when faced with a situation you cannot control, to admit you can do nothing. -- Lemony Snicket

Ineffective Treatment #6: Psychotherapy and Psychoanalysis

There are several studies where psychotherapy has been used to treat personality disorders. Unfortunately, most of them are very poorly designed (32). This means that they did not do a professional job with diagnosing, or with keeping records of the therapy sessions, or with the follow-up of their patients. Some studies didn't have a good way to measure improvement (one study simply asked the patients, "Do you feel more empathic?"). Some were measuring things that had little to do with personality disorders (one study included only Avoidant Personality Disorder patients, and measured only if it was easier for them to leave the house, not how successfully they were able to interact with people) (32).

Most of these very dubious studies report wonderful recovery rates for their subjects, sometimes as high as 60%. This sounds refreshingly promising and very hopeful, until we look a little closer at the studies.

One of the most dismal weaknesses in theoe studies was diagnosing. Scientists and doctors want to be right, just like everyone else. They want to succeed and help people. They are human, and are just as prone to wishful thinking as the little kindergartener who stands on his tip-toes and implores, "Look how BIG I am! I'm as tall as my DAD!" We nod, and smile, and agree. If scientists do it, Aunt Alex finds this wishful thinking a bit less cute. They should know better. They should be more careful. So, if they are conducting research, studying whether their subjects are improved or even cured by their treatment, they had better be extremely consistent in their diagnosing criteria. Quite frankly, one of the best ways to determine for sure if someone is personality-disordered is to interview their family and associates as well as the patient. Narcissists will lie; their exhausted and emotionally battered family members usually do not. Narcissists will edit events, feelings and behaviors until they are unrecognizable. Family members are much less likely to do so. Families want a reality check. Narcissists want nothing to do with reality. If you wish to study personality-disordered people, relying solely on the reports and answers of the patients is woefully lacking in scientific strength.

A particularly disappointing example of this was a study where the researching psychologist spent several months working with a borderline patient. Some months after they ended the therapy, he happened to see his patient in a museum. He reported in his research that for that twenty minutes in which he chatted with her at the museum, she appeared relaxed, cheerful, and sociable, and completely appropriate in her behavior (42).

He promptly recorded her as cured.

I am not making this up.

Books and studies and many reputable articles in scientific journals were found and closely reviewed by Aunt Alex. A popular topic was why it is so hard even to put together a study that can look closely at narcissism, because getting narcissists to look at themselves, report their thoughts and feelings honestly, question their grandiosity, and work toward meaningful change are all things that fly directly in the face of the mental disorder they hold so dear (Ronningstam, 2011). In a cage match between their personality disorder and the desire for a happy life, the disorder will win every time.

The research studied people with personality disorders who were treated with psychotherapy. Most studies reported a success rate of zero. The rest of them -- all of them -- had serious research design flaws. For instance, another study noted that therapies that were used to treat personality disorders actually were treating symptoms, like phobias or mania (3).

  Number of narcissists treated with psychotherapy who are reported to have developed empathy, or increased insight, or ceased manipulation, or ceased lying, or ceased idealization and devaluation cycles in their relationships: **Zero. Not one**.

Practice non-interference. Wait for others to seek a remedy rather than forcing it upon them.
-- Lao Tzu, Tao Te Ching (translation by Richard Degen)

Ineffective Treatment #7: Psychodrama

  Lucy Griffith has proposed using psychodrama to treat personality disorders, with schema therapy used in therapy groups as well (13). This is much like skill building, as the patients are acting out, or practicing, conduct in scripted situations. Personality-disordered group members act out and test certain responses in anxiety-evoking scenes. Mental health professionals may also say that the participation in the mini-dramas allow narcissists to act out their 'schemas', or 'traumatic pasts', or 'experiential paradigms', or whatever they want to call 'hang-ups' in their favorite lingo. Psychodrama sounds fun, but it's not particularly effective.

  A key assumption of Ms. Griffith's psychodrama treatment is that people form their own personalities, and therefore personalities can be molded by a person, as long as they really want to do so (13). This is -- how can I say this respectfully? I cannot -- **It is ridiculous**. Further, the group setting of psychodrama sessions isn't of terrific benefit, because narcissists, antisocial types, borderline types, etc., are not pack animals. They do not naturally form groups, or interact equitably. Narcissists are likely to manipulate and use each other just as readily as they do the mentally healthy. They're not good at mutual support or cooperation, any more than they are at supporting or collaborating with their family or associates.

Examples in the scientific literature of successful recovery cases, or improvement in behavior (impulse control problems, lying, absurd mood swings, irrational thinking, etc.), in narcissists using psychodrama: **None**.

****

Well, now that we're thoroughly demoralized and our hopes have been summarily dashed, let's see what's going on here, and whether we ourselves can maybe invent a way to cure narcissism. Heck, if it can be done, Aunt Alex's Army is more than willing to help with the effort. So, let's see if trying to fix a toad is a good use of our time.

The DSM-IV approach

If we're going to treat a malady, we need to know what the heck it is. Among the members of the Guild of Mental Health Professionals, the DSM-IV rules the diagnostic roost. DSM stands for Diagnostic and Statistical Manual of Mental Disorders (1). It undergoes irregular updates and revisions, roughly at the rate which doctors and scientists change their minds about things.

A great deal of intelligence can be invested in ignorance when the need for illusion is deep. --Saul Bellow

The DSM is divided up into sections. One section has mental illnesses like depression, bipolar disorder, and schizophrenia. The second section has only two parts: mental retardation, and personality disorders. This is for a good reason. Both mental retardation and personality disorders are permanent.   Patients don't change, they don't get cured, and the conditions always affect **all** of their thoughts, feelings, and behaviors. Always. Both mental retardation and personality disorders are rigid, intransigent, unbudging parts of the person's being. They are set off in a section all to themselves because they have so much in common. And in terms of curability, the things they have in common aren't good. The one major difference between the mentally retarded and the personality disordered is awareness. Many persons with mental retardation know about their disability and are aware of the differences it makes. Not so the narcissist. He doesn't see a disorder inside himself. He thinks everyone is as screwed up as he is. (This little factoid also contributes to the impossibility of curing a narcissist. If we talk with him about treatment for his personality disorder, he feels like we just want to weaken him so that we can dominate and manipulate him more easily.)

It is the responsibility of intellectuals to speak the truth and expose lies.
- Noam Chomsky

A special mention of empathy

Across populations and cultures, for all people, there's a regard for the needs and well-being of others, particularly the vulnerable -- children, the sick, and the elderly. This regard for the well-being of others is part of our success as a species. When other people are in pain, healthy people find that to be unpleasant. The needs of others are of interest to healthy people. And when interests compete, such as when buying or bartering, healthy people are able to resolve the competing issues, most of the time. People generally don't lie to each other without urgent cause, or invade each other's space, or manipulate one another. Empathy is an extremely complex, and extremely beautiful, weave of instinct, behavior, bonding, and feeling.

The stark lack of empathy is a major component of what makes it impossible to have a relationship with a narcissist. To the personality-disordered, it's a zero-sum game: The more they have to take the interests of others into consideration, the less care they can give to their own interests. So, helping another means destroying himself. This handicap, this deficit in empathy, can't be reversed, and empathy doesn't magically appear after years of selfish, hateful anxiety, like it can in the movies. Schema therapy can't help with empathy, because it's not a schema issue. Empathy isn't a skill you can learn. Narcissists can learn to mimic some behaviors that normal people usually use when they're being empathic and compassionate. But to regard this as a psychological and behavioral twin to true empathy is like announcing that pictures of food are as nourishing as the real thing.

Getting real: The brain damage

The bare-bones best redress for those involved with narcissists is to get away from them. Never enable their bad behavior or indulge their manipulations. Stay away from them completely. This is the best thing for them, and for you. Changing life-long personality traits even in a healthy person is a Herculean task. In a narcissist his traits aren't just a long-standing problem, but they are also held by him with the tightest of grips.

Narcissists are hell-bent on changing others, not themselves, and can be very slippery about it. Their delusional rationalizations can boggle the mind. This approach doesn't change when the narcissist enters any kind of therapy or treatment. They don't take a break from being mentally ill in order to engage the treatment. They tell themselves the therapist is trying to make them boring, or that she is calling them a liar, or she doesn't understand him. So, their mental illness is pretty much fatal to successful therapy. Their failure in interpersonal interactions, probably why they are in therapy, is the very failure that makes it impossible to establish an effective relationship with the therapist (33). This causes a mobius-strip situation in which the therapist cannot help the patient until the patient has resolved the interpersonal problem for which he's seeing the therapist in the first place.

The big picture is even more bleak. One cannot wish away, or talk away, or medicate away, brain damage. Trying harder doesn't help (not that the narcissist would try harder, even if it would.) More on the brain damage in a bit.

Families need to know this in order to make sense of the past and in order to plan wisely and sanely for the future. As with many chronic medical conditions, the families of the patients know a whole lot more about the condition than many doctors and scientists. Narcissism is no exception. Some mental health professionals are so eager to have robust results, that they are vulnerable to a logical fallacy: Therapies and treatments work on non-narcissistic people with bad childhoods. Narcissists had bad childhoods. Therefore, treatment and therapies will be effective with narcissists.

The error is the assumption that non-narcissists and narcissists will respond equally effectively to any given treatment. This is preposterous. Narcissists edit their childhood experiences, current behaviors, and thoughts in therapy just as heavily as they do everywhere else, and this makes the therapy process a fractured and faulty waste of time.

Some mental health professionals who work with narcissistic patients report that one of the strengths of their particular therapy is that their therapy normalizes rather than pathologizes personality disorders. The puzzling implication here is that there is no real benefit to recognizing severe disorders as pathological. Personality disorders are not normal. Irrational thinking, self-hate, and knee-jerk reactivity aren't healthy. Pretending they are normal doesn't make them so. It only further enables the narcissist.

Our greatest pretenses are built up not to hide the evil and the ugly in us, but our emptiness. The hardest thing to hide is something that is not there. --Eric Hoffer

Meaningful medical and clinical recovery means that the patient no longer meets criteria for their illness or disorder. In the case of narcissists, if they've recovered, they can function much more normally, and aren't in danger of lapsing back into toad mode at any given moment. Here's what the scientific literature reports: Recovery has never happened with a narcissist. The goal of any good therapy is to get the client to his or her own "a-ha!" moment, which is an awareness that leads to meaningful change and increased quality of life. Is this reasonable to expect from a population that is starkly poor at self-reflection? Isn't it a better, more dignified approach for narcissist, therapist, and family alike, to stay firmly grounded in reality regarding their ability to get better? We accept that developmentally delayed people are going to have cognitive limitations all their lives, and this acceptance helps us to serve them more appropriately and more to their benefit. It helps us to understand them and be realistic about what they are and are not able to do. Why should our approach to personality disorders be any different?

If we frequently break agreements -- whether with others or with ourselves -- we are training ourselves to ignore our own word. Committing to [anything] is about as significant as saying we will learn to fly -- sounds nice, would be fun, but it's not going to happen. Committing ... is not a one-time occurrence. It must be done daily, hourly, continually. We must CHOOSE to commit to our CHOICE, over and over.
-- Peter McWilliams

Some folks want to believe (and who can blame them) that personality disorders can be fixed, and these are the same folks who point to childhood abuse as the cause of the narcissist's totally messed-up head. Therefore, since the damage was caused by experiences, we can use treatments to help the patient overcome them and resolve them. As we mentioned before, it's easy to believe that almost all narcissists had abusive childhoods, but this doesn't mean the bad childhood caused the disorder. It means that because personality disorders are inherited and are deeply embedded in a person's DNA, then it's pretty doggone likely that one (or both) of the narcissist's parents were personality disordered too, and, hence, pretty crappy parents. Personality disordered parents are extremely unlikely to provide nourishing and attentive environments for their kids. This causes awful childhoods, but it doesn't cause personality disorders. A child with the DNA for a personality disorder is going to have a personality disorder, no matter how saintly their parents are, or how wonderful their upbringing.

You don't have to wait for someone to treat you badly repeatedly. All it takes is once, and if they get away with it that once, if they know they can treat you like that, then it sets the pattern for the future. -- Jane Green

      In narcissists and other personality disordered people, it's all reacting and not much thinking. Narcissists live their lives moving from one knee-jerk response to the next, all based on what they want right that second, and what they're perceiving as threats right that second. They're always thinking with the primitive, fight-flight-or-freeze part of their brain, rather than the rational, organized part. This will never change, because we can't strengthen the rational part enough for it to master control over the reactive, primitive part. The rational part is too flimsy.

      The domination of this reactive, primitive part of the brain over the thinking part is also seen in people with serious addiction problems. The addiction becomes very emotional for them -- they "need" their drink or their fix, and are willing to do any number of impulsive, criminal, or just dumb things to get it. Thinking clearly and rationally takes a back seat. The difference, though, is that addicts (who don't also have a personality disorder) usually have an intact, functioning thinking part of their brain, which <u>can</u> be strengthened back into its dominant role of running the show.

This primitive-thinking-is-the-boss situation inside the narcissist's head also explains why their lives are so desperate. If their defenses, the extremely obnoxious and intolerable behaviors they use to lash out, were suddenly (or gradually) taken away, the narcissist would be left with a reality of pure roiling, unbearable pain. Unbearable psychological pain is at the root of all of the narcissist's bad behavior; it is so excruciating that it sometimes feels to them like body pain as well. People with personality disorders feel pain most of the time, and to them it feels like it's coming from all sides. They're terrified and mad and frustrated almost all of the time, like a person in fight-flight-or-freeze mode, 24/7. They seek to give themselves a moment's respite from this torment in almost everything they think, say and do. Whether it's being an obsessive control freak because he's feeling scattered, or pretending to be powerful because he's feeling weak, or manipulating you into reassuring him that he's fabulous because he's hating himself, it's all about his desperate and neverending mission to keep his head together. This is tragic, and can be heartbreaking, if the narcissist is your child or loved one. But it's not something over which to throw your own life away. It's like a beloved dog who gets rabies -- you can love him from a distance, but continuing to let him sleep in your bed or play with your kids is just a bad idea.

On the train of can-do, he's the brake pedal.
-- Anonymous

And now we get to the meat of the matter, the reality that puts all else into focus.

Buried deep within the medical journals, whispered in the locked, smoky back rooms of psychology conferences all over the world, is the truth: People with personality disorders are born with brain damage. You're not dealing with a guy who's misunderstood, or eccentric, or "difficult". He's not even really mentally ill, in the traditional sense of the term. He's brain damaged. The damage was caused by bad wiring in his DNA.

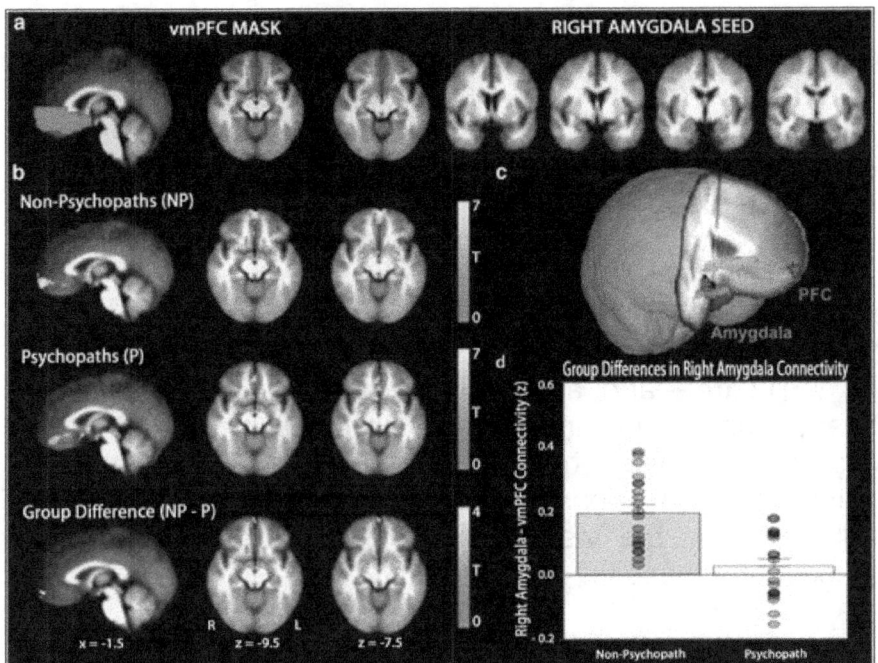

Figure 2

Functional connectivity between the right amygdala and anterior vmPFC is reduced in psychopaths. *a*, Group differences in connectivity were assessed in the vmPFC mask (red) for correlation coefficients computed using the mean time series extracted from the hand drawn right amygdala seed (blue). *b*, Mean right amygdala–vmPFC connectivity maps for non-psychopaths and psychopaths are shown separately on the group mean anatomical image, thresholded at a cluster corrected $p < 0.05$. Scale bars depict the uncorrected *t* statistic. Both groups exhibit significant resting connectivity between right amygdala and regions of vmPFC. The group difference map indicates an area in anterior vmPFC where non-psychopaths have significantly greater connectivity than psychopaths ($x = -3$, $y = -66$, $z = -10$, cluster size = 14 voxels). *c*, A three-dimensional rendering of the group mean anatomical image shows the location of the amygdala seed (blue) and significant vmPFC cluster (red) in relation to the UF (green). *d*, The bar plot depicts the significant group difference in connectivity estimates (Fisher z-transformed correlation coefficients) within the vmPFC cluster. Error bars indicate SEM. Filled circles represent values from individual subjects.

Reduced Prefrontal Connectivity in Psychopathy
J Neurosci. 2011 November 30;31(48):17348-17357.

(A) Slide from the study by Motzkin JC, Newman JP, Kiehl KA, and Koenigs M: Reduced Prefrontal Connectivity in Psychopathy.

The scientists and doctors are continuing to study inborn brain damage, and are finding evidence left and right of its relationship to psychopathy and personality disorders. Doctors have used MRI (magnetic resonance imaging) to peek at the brains of antisocial types, and have found a significant reduction in the gray matter in their prefrontal cortex (27). They have also found that in the presence of an emotional stressor, there is less neuron activity in that part of the brain (34). This makes sense, as one of the creepiest things about people with antisocial personality disorder (and narcissists, and avoidant types) is how flat their responses can be in situations involving other people. It's as though someone threw a wet blanket on the spark of their ability to have compassion, concern, and involvement. It's as though they don't care -- and, as it turns out, they don't. Those human, soulful sparks in their brains aren't firing. It also explains why they can have such a ridiculously difficult time making simple decisions, much less the hard ones. With tough decisions, the vast majority of narcissists just escape, and leave the mess for others to manage.

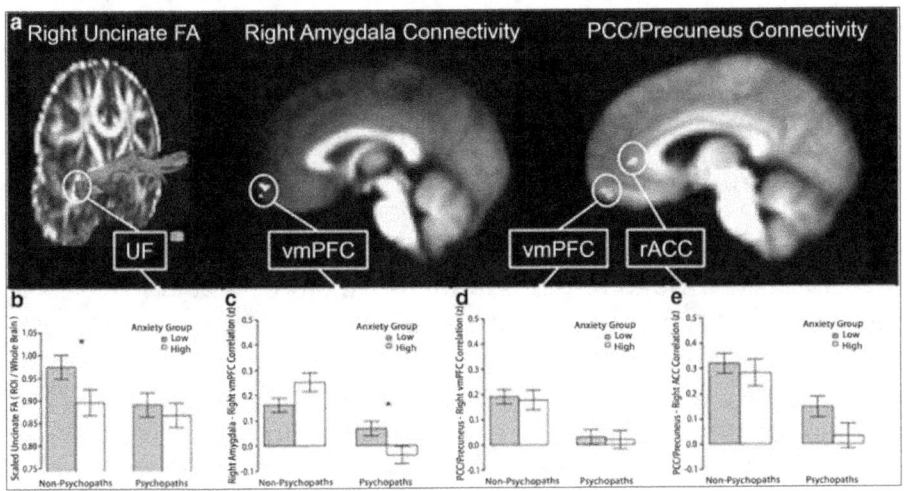

Figure 4

Analysis of DTI and rest-fMRI findings with respect to psychopathy subtype. *a*, Depiction of each significant finding in the main between-group analyses (psychopaths vs nonpsychopaths). *b*, For right UF FA values, among non-psychopaths, the low- and high-anxious subgroups significantly differ ($p = 0.046$); there is no such difference among psychopaths. *c*, For the cluster identified in the right amygdala–vmPFC connectivity analysis, there is a significant interaction between psychopathy and anxiety ($p = 0.005$), indicating that connectivity is differentially modulated by anxiety subgroup in psychopaths and non-psychopaths. *d*, *e*, There are no significant interactions between psychopathy and anxiety for medial parietal–vmPFC connectivity. Error bars indicate SEM. Asterisks indicate significant differences between anxiety subtypes.

Reduced Prefrontal Connectivity in Psychopathy
J Neurosci. 2011 November 30;31(48):17348-17357.

(B) Slide from the study by Motzkin JC, Newman JP, Kiehl KA, and Koenigs M: Reduced Prefrontal Connectivity in Psychopathy.

Scientists also suspect the impulse control issues found in people with personality disorders are due to this brain impairment (49). It takes more brain function to stop and think than it does to react impulsively.

There's your evidence, dear reader. Contrary to their desperate claims otherwise, they really are defective.

Behold: Sato and his colleagues found that the superior temporal sulcus/gyrus (bilateral) part of the brain had noticeably less gray matter in psychopaths (39). Motzkin and his colleagues showed reduced white matter connecting the anterior temporal lobes and the prefrontal cortex in psychopaths (27). Ermer and his colleagues used MRI and found decreased volumes of gray matter in the orbitofrontal cortex, bilateral temporal poles, and posterior cingulate cortex in the brains of psychopath (7). They call this reduced volume a "neural dysfunction", and relate it directly to psychopathic traits -- which include no empathy, hurting others, manipulating, and lying. Yang and his associates took this a step further (51), and used brain imagery to find that the greater the brain damage, the stupider the psychopath -- and the more likely he is to get caught. (OK, Aunt Alex is paraphrasing a bit here. The actual journal article calls the toads with greater brain damage "unsuccessful psychopaths", i.e., the ones more likely to get caught.) The "unsuccessful" psychopaths had even less gray matter in the frontal cortex and amygdala areas of the brain, predisposing them to poor behavior and bad decision-making.

The narcissist? He speaks the loudest when he is silent. He says, "I use people. I have no use for you right this second."
-- Aunt Alex

The list goes on. Narcissists walk, and talk, and usually can do simple math, but now we have proof -- they're brain damaged. And that congenital brain damage makes them uselessly bad at interpersonal relationships. It makes them really bad at organizing their thoughts and feelings. It makes them hurt other people just to feel safe. The missing tissue in their brains is the stuff that, in normal people, allows us to modulate our emotions, care about other people, think in layers, appreciate subtlety, and calm ourselves. Those areas of our brains allow us to develop values, and assess our fear and anxiety. They let us organize our feelings. They allow us to bond and to love, and appreciate being loved.

What does this mean for you? It means that it's safe to let go of your hope for fixing narcissists, and to love them from a distance, just like you would any other psychopath. It means you'll never have a satisfying conversation with them where you feel heard and understood. It means you'll never feel like you'll have closure with them, either, because they don't really understand the human need for that.

The word 'busy' is a load of crap in relationships. It seems like a good excuse, but all you have is a man who didn't care enough to call. Remember, men are never too busy to get what they want.
-- Greg Behrendt

There are people who have written love letters to convicts such as Charles Manson, and Scott Peterson (convicted murderer of Laci and Conner Peterson), and Richard Ramirez, and Ted Bundy. There are people who spend years, decades, tolerating (and even enabling) the bad behavior of narcissists, deciding it's working for them (though it absolutely isn't) or that someday it will get better (though it absolutely won't). Some people are pretty sure toads only need to be loved, or need psychiatric care, or need to be valued for who they are, and then life with them will be fulfilling, nourishing, peaceful, and good. But the troops in Aunt Alex's Army know better. They do not suffer kindly the rancid machinations of toads. The troops find that pairing up with someone who's abusive, and/or an emotional mess, and/or a psychopath, is really a bad idea.

Clarity and serenity should be at the root of all action.
-- Lao Tzu, Tao Te Ching (translation by Richard Degen)

References

1. American Psychiatric Association. (2000). <u>Diagnostic and statistical manual of mental disorders (4th ed., rev.).</u> Washington DC: Author.

2. Babiak P, Neumann CS, Hare RD (2010). Corporate psychopathy: Talking the walk. <u>Behavioral Sciences and the Law, 28</u>(2), 174-93.

3. Ball SA, Young JE (2000). Dual Focus Schema Therapy for Personality Disorders and Substance Dependence: Case Study Results. <u>Cognitive and Behavioral Practice, 7</u>, 270-281.

4. Bamber M (2004). The Good, the Bad and Defenceless Jimmy -- A single case study of schema mode therapy. <u>Clinical Psychology and Psychotherapy, 11</u>, 425-438.

5. Bernstein DP (2002). Cognitive therapy of personality disorders in patients with histories of emotional abuse or neglect. <u>Psychiatric Annals, 32</u>(10), 618-628.

6. Collard P (2004). Interview with Jeffrey Young: reinventing your life through schema therapy. <u>Counseling Psychology Quarterly, 17</u>(1), 1-11.

7. Ermer E, Cope LM, Nyalakanti PK, Calhoun VD, Kiehl KA (2013). Aberrant paralimbic gray matter in incarcerated male adolescents with psychopathic traits. <u>Journal of the American Academy of Child and Adolescent Psychiatry, 52</u>(1):94-103.

8. Fonagy P (2000). Attachment and Borderline Personality Disorder. <u>Journal of the American Psychoanalytical Association, 48</u>(4), 1129-1146.

9. Fromm E (1973). <u>The Anatomy of Human Destructiveness.</u> Holt, Rinehart & Winston, New York.

10. Ford CV, King BH, Hollender MH (1988). Lies and liars: psychiatric aspects of prevarication. <u>American Journal of Psychiatry, 145</u>(5), 554-62.

11. Gabbard GO (2000). Psychotherapy of personality disorders. <u>Journal of Psychotherapy Practice and Research, 9,</u> 1-6.

12. Glantz K, Goisman RM (1990). Relaxation and merging in the treatment of personality disorders. <u>American Journal of Psychotherapy, 44</u>(3), 405-413.

13. Griffith LF (2003). Combining Schema-Focused Cognitive Therapy and Psychodrama: A Model for Treating Clients With Personality Disorders. <u>Journal of Group Psychotherapy, Psychodrama, & Sociometry, 55 </u>(4), 128-   140.

14. Gunderson JG, Ronningstam E (2001). Differentiating narcissistic and antisocial personality disorders. <u>Journal of Personality Disorders, 15</u>(2), 103-9.

15. Hare RD (1999). <u>Without Conscience: The Disturbing World of the Psychopaths Among Us.</u> Guilford Press, New York.

16. Hare RD, Neumann CS (2010). The role of antisociality in the psychopathy construct: comment on Skeen and Cooke (2010). <u>Psychological Assessment, 22</u>(2), 446-454.

17. Hare RD, Neumann CS (2009). Psychopathy: assessment and forensic implications. <u>Canadian Journal of Psychiartry, 54</u>(12), 791-802.

18. Herve HF, Hayes PJ, Hare RD (2003). Psychopathy and sensitivity to the emotional polarity of metaphorical

statements. Personality and Individual Differences, 35, 1497-1507.

19. Horney K (1950). Neurosis and Human Growth: The Struggle toward Self-realization. W.W. Norton & Company, New York.

20. James IA (2001). Schema Therapy: The next generation, but should it carry a health warning? Behavioural and Cognitive Psychotherapy, 29, 401-407.

21. Karterud S, Oien M, Pedersen G (2011). Validity aspects of the Diagnostic and Statistical Manual of Mental Disorders, Fourth Edition, narcissistic personality disorder construct. Comparative Psychiatry, 52(5), 517-26.

22. Kluger J (2003). Masters of denial. Time, 161(3), 84.

23. Livesley JW (1993). Genetic and environmental conributions to dimensions of personality disorder. American Journal of Psychiatry, 150(12), 1826-1831.

24. Livesley JW (2003). Practical Management of Personality Disorders. Guilford Press, New York.

25. Lobbestael J, Arnts A, Sieswerda S (2005). Schema modes and childhood abuse in borderline and antisocial personality disorders. Journal of Behavior Therapy and Experimental Psychiatry, 36, 240-253.

26. Maslow AH (1968). Toward a Psychology of Being. Van Nostrand Reinhold Publishing, New York.

27. Motzkin JC, Newman JP, Kiehl KA, Koenigs M (2011). Reduced prefrontal connectivity in psychopathy. Journal of Neuroscience, 31(48), 17348-17357.

28. Moser S, Dereczyk A (2012). Predicting physician assistant students' professionalism by personality attributes. Journal of Physician Assistant Education, 23(3), 28-32.

29. Newton-Howes G, Tyrer P (2003). Pharmacotherapy for personality disorders. Expert Opinions in Pharmacotherapy, 4(10), 1643-1649.

30. Nordahl HM, Nysaeter TE (2005). Schema therapy for patients with borderline personality disorder: a single case series. Journal of Behavior Therapy and Experimental Psychiatry, 36, 254-264.

31. Paris J (1998). Psychotherapy for the personality disorders: Working with traits. Bulletin of the Menninger Clinic, 65(3), 287-97.

32. Perry JC, Banon E, Ianni F (1999). Effectiveness of psychotherapy for personality disorders. American Journal of Psychiatry, 156(9), 1312-1321.

33. Persons JB, Bertagnolli A (1994). Cognitive-behavioral treatment of multiple-problem patients: Application to personality disorders. Clinical Psychology and Psychotherapy, 1(5), 279-285.

34. Raine A, Lencz T, Bihrle S, LaCasse L, Colletti P (2000). Reduced prefrontal gray matter volume and reduced autonomic activity in antisocial personality disorder. Archives of General Psychiatry, 57(2), 119-129.

35. Rivas-Vazquez RA, Blais M (2002). Pharmacologic treatment of personality disorders. Professional Psychology: Research and Practice, 33(1), 104-107.

36. Rizvi SL, Linehan MM (2001). Dialectical behavior therapy for personality disorders. Current Psychiatry Reports, 3(1), 64-9.

37. Ronningstam E (2012). Alliance building and narcissistic personality disorder. Journal of Clinical Psychology, 68(8), 943-53.

38. Ryden G, Vinnars B (2002). Pharmacological treatment of borderline personality disorders. Lakartidningen, 99(50), 5088-5094.

39. Sato JR, de Oliviera-Souza R, Thomaz CE, Basilio R, Bramati IE, Amaro Jr E, Tovar-Moll F, Hare RD, Moll J (2011). Identification of psychopathic individuals using pattern classification of MRI images. Society of Neuroscience, 6(5-6), 627-639.

40. Soloff P (1997). Psychobiologic perspectives on treatment of personality disorders. Journal of Personality Disorders, 11(4), 336-344.

41. Stanley B, Bundy E, Beberman R (2001). Skills training as an adjunctive treatment for personality disorders. Journal of Psychiatric Practice, 7(5), 324-335.

42. Stone MH (2003). Borderline patients at the border of treatability: At the intersection of borderline, narcissistic, and antisocial personalities. Journal of Psychiatric Practice, 9(4), 279-291.

43. Svartberg M, Stiles TC, Seltzer MH (2004). Randomized, controlled trial of the effectiveness of short-term dynamic psychotherapy and cognitive therapy for Cluster C personality disorders. American Journal of Psychiatry, 161, 810-817.

44. Target M (1998). Outcome research on the psychosocial treatment of personality disorders. Bulletin of the Menninger Clinic, 62(2), 215-231.

45. Tredget JE (2001). The aetiology, presentation and treatment of personality disorders. Journal of Psychiatric and Mental Health Nursing, 8, 347-356.

46. Trestman RL (2004). Optimism grows for combined treatment of severe personality disorders. Psychiatric Times, 21, 35-40.

47. Tyrer P, Mitchard S, Methuen C, Ranger M (2003). Treatment rejecting and treatment seeking personality disorders: Type R and Type S. Journal of Personality Disorders, 17(3), 263-268.

48. Vanaerschot G (2004). It takes two to tango: On empathy with fragile processes. Psychotherapy: Theory, Research, Practice, Training, 41(2), 112-124.

49. Vollm B, Richardson P, Stirling J, Elliot R, Dolan M, Chaudhry I, Delben C, McKie S, Anderson I, Deakin B (2004). Neurobiological substrates of antisocial and borderline personality disorder: preliminary results of a functional fMRI study. Criminal Behaviour and Mental Health, 14, 39–54.

50. Villernarette-Pittman NR, Stanford MS, Greve KW, Houston RJ, Mathias CW (2004). Obsessive-Compulsive Personality Disorder and behavioral disinhibition. Journal of Psychology, 138(1), 5-23.

51. Yang Y, Raine A, Colletti P, Toga AW, Narr KL (2010). Morphological alterations in the prefrontal cortex and the amygdala in unsuccessful psychopaths. Journal of Abnormal Psychology, 19(3), 546-554.

52. Young JE, Behary WT (1998). Schema-focused therapy for personality disorders. In Treating complex cases: The cognitive behavioural therapy approach. Tarrier, N & Wells, A et al., (Eds), p. 340-376. John Wiley & Sons, Ltd., New York, NY; 1998.

53. Young JE, Flanagan C (1998). Schema-focused therapy for narcissistic patients. In <u>Disorders of narcissism: Diagnostic, clinical, and empirical implications</u>. Ronningstam, EF (Ed), p. 239-262. American Psychiatric Association, 1998.

54. Young JE (2003). <u>Schema Therapy: A Practitioner's Guide.</u> The Guilford Press, New York.